No._____

In the

Supreme Court of the United States

Thomas G. Jewusiak, *Petitioner*

v.

Sandy Kaye Condominium Association, Inc.,
Respondents

On Petition for Writ of Certiorari to the Florida Fifth
District Court of Appeal

PETITION FOR WRIT OF CERTIORARI

Thomas G. Jewusiak
P.O. Box 33794
Indialantic Florida 32903
321-292-2450
Jewusiak1@aol.com

May 29, 2012

Revised July 31, 2012

(i)

Questions Presented

1. Whether a citizen of the United States, can have his property seized, his only home taken, the product of his whole life's work, without "due process" of law, in violation of the Constitution of the United States.
2. Whether the refusal by the lower courts in this particular case, to observe the careful strictures of summary judgment established by *Celotex, Matushita* and *Anderson* and their myriad progeny, represents a particularly egregious abuse of the Constitutional due process rights of the petitioner.
3. Furthermore and separately, whether Summary Judgment is itself so fraught with peril for potential abuse of the Constitution of the United States that its safeguards should be strengthened. And whether the Fifth District Court of Appeals of Florida and other courts of appeal should be required to enter an opinion in a case such as this, in which a person's total life savings, (equity of $500,000), his only home, is, in effect, seized by the lower court, acting for the Sandy Kaye Condominium Association in a manufactured dispute resulting in a "special" assessment for window caulking for which the petitioner was singled out.

Parties to the Proceedings

Thomas G. Jewusiak, pro se,

Petitioner

Sandy Kaye Condominium Association, Inc.

Respondent

Represented by: Lilliana M. Farinas-Sabogal, Esq., Becker & Poliakoff, 121 Alhambra Plaza, Suite 1000, Miami, Florida 33134

(iii)

Table of Contents

QUESTIONS PRESENTED..................................(i)

PARTIES TO THE PROCEEDING.....................(ii)

TABLE OF CONTENTS............................(iii)-(iv)

TABLE OF AUTHORITIES.........................(v)-(vii)

PETITION FOR CERTIORARI.............................1

OPINIONS BELOW..2

JURISDICTION...3

CONSTITUTIONAL PROVISIONS INVOLVED......5

STATEMENT OF THE CASE...........................6-23

ARGUMENTS...23-27

PROOF OF THE ARGUMENTS.....................28-34

CONCLUSION...35

APPENDIX: pgs. 1-30

1. Order of the Eighteenth Judicial Circuit in and for Brevard County, Florida, Case No 05-2006-CA-052659 denying Thomas Jewusiak's demand for jury trial, discovery and sufficient

(iv)

time for trial; denied without citation of law or legal rationale by the lower tribunal for violating the Constitution; filed Feb. 26, 2009. .... Appendix pg. 1-2

2. Order of the Eighteenth Judicial Circuit in and for Brevard County, Florida, Case No 05-2006-CA-052659 granting Sandy Kaye motion for Final Summary Judgment without the lower tribunal citing any case law or legal basis for granting summary judgment, filed June 10, 2009......................Appendix pg. 3-17

3. Order of the Eighteenth Judicial Circuit in and for Brevard County, Florida, Case No 05-2006-CA-052659 granting Sandy Kaye Motion to Reset Foreclosure Sale, filed Aug. 18, 2009 .... Appendix pg. 19-21

4. Order of the Eighteenth Judicial Circuit in and for Brevard County, Florida, Case No 05-2006-CA-052659 granting Sandy Kaye Motion to Reset Foreclosure Sale, filed December 4, 2010 .... Appendix pg. 23-24

5. Order of the Fifth District Court of Appeal of Florida, Per Curiam, Affirmed, filed Jan. 31, 2012 .... Appendix pg. 25

6. Order of the Fifth District Court of Appeal, Motion for Rehearing, Clarification, denied, filed Feb. 15, 2012 .... Appendix pg. 27

7. Notice of Dismissal for lack of jurisdiction, Supreme Court of Florida dated May 1, 2012 .... Appendix pg. 29-30

Table of Authorities

FED. R.CIV. P. 56(c)..30

FED. R.CIV. P. 56(e)..30

FED. R.CIV. P. 56(e)(1)......................................30

MOORE'S FED. PRACTICE ¶ 56.22[1], at 56-1312 to 56-1316 (2d ed. 1985)..29

FEDERAL RULES OF EVIDENCE...............29, 33

Alpert v. United States, 481 F.3d 404, 409 (6th Cir. 2007)..30

Anderson v. Liberty Lobby, Inc., 477 US 242 Supreme Court (1986) 31

Anderson v. United States, 417 U.S. Supreme Court (1974)..31

Argo v. Blue Cross & Blue Shield of Kan., Inc., 452 F.3d 1193, 1199 (10th Cir.2006)..........................30

Beyah v. Coughlin, 789 F.2d 986, 989 (2d Cir. 1986)...29

Bolen v. Dengel, 340 F.3d 300, 313 (5th Cir. 2003)..30

Celotex Corp. v. Catrett, 477 U.S. 317, 323, 106 S.Ct. 2548, 91 L.Ed.2d 265 (1986)..........................28, 31

Goguen v. Textron, Inc., 234 F.R.D. 13, 16 (D. Mass. 2006)..29

Hardy v. S.F. Phosphates Ltd. Co., 185 F.3d 1076, 1082 n.5 (10th Cir.1999).....................................30

Jenkins v. Winter, 540 F.3d 742, 748 (8th Cir. 2008)..29

Macuba v. Deboer, 193 F. 3d 1316 Court of Appeals, (11th Cir. 1999)..30

Major League Baseball Props. v. Salvino, Inc., 542 F.3d 290, 310 (2d Cir. 2008).............................29

Matsushita Elec. Industrial Co. v. Zenith Radio Corp., 475 US 574 - Supreme Court 1986.............33

United States v. $92,203.00 in U.S. Currency, 537 F.3d 504, 508 (5th Cir. 2008)............................29

Ward v. Int'l Paper Co., 509 F.3d 457, 462 (8th Cir. 2007)..30

Wiley v. United States, 20 F.3d 222, 226 (6th Cir. 1994)..29

Other Authorities

Jay Daigneault, *Constitutional Law: Due Process* 34 Stetson L. Rev. 829 (2004-2005)..........................4

James Joseph Duane, *The Four Greatest Myths About Summary Judgment*, 52 Wash. & Lee L. Rev. 1523 (1995)...31, 32, 32

Paul Mollica , *Federal Summary Judgment at High Tide,* 84 Marq. L. Rev. Rev. 141-142 (2000)

William W. Schwarzer, Alan Hirsch & David J. Barrans, *The Analysis & Decision of Summary Judgment Motions: A Monograph on Rule 56 of the Federal Rules of Civil Procedure*, 139 F.R.D. 441, 481 (1992)...31

Bradley Scott Shannon, *"Should Summary Judgment be Granted?"* American University Law Review 58, no. 1 (October 2008): 85-126. 31

Adam N. Steinman, *The Irrepressible Myth of Celotex: Reconsidering Summary Judgment Burdens Twenty Years After The Trilogy* 63 Wash. & Lee L. Rev. 81 (2006)

Stern, Gressman, Shapiro & Geller, *Supreme Court Practice* (7th ed. 1993)

PETITION FOR CERTIORARI

This case offers this Court a vehicle to resolve pressing and persistent questions and apparent contradictions in the understanding of the limits of summary judgment and the Constitutional perils involved in its misinterpretation and misuse. It also affords this Court the opportunity to right a terrible wrong committed against one family.

Opinions Below

1.   Order of the Eighteenth Judicial Circuit in and for Brevard County, Florida, Case No 05-2006-CA-052659 denying Thomas Jewusiak's demand for jury trial, discovery and sufficient time for trial; denied without citation of law or legal rationale provided by the lower tribunal; filed Feb. 26, 2009. The "demand" for jury trial raised the constitutional issue.

2.   Order of the Eighteenth Judicial Circuit in and for Brevard County, Florida, Case No 05-2006-CA-052659 granting Sandy Kaye motion for Final Summary Judgment, filed June 10, 2009; filed without citation of law or legal rationale for granting summary judgment but rather the lower tribunal issued findings of fact which are beyond the proper scope of summary judgment; violations of the 7th and 14th amendments.

3.   Order of the Eighteenth Judicial Circuit in and for Brevard County, Florida, Case No 05-2006-CA-052659 granting Sandy Kaye Motion to Reset Foreclosure Sale, filed Aug. 18, 2009.

4.   Order of the Eighteenth Judicial Circuit in and for Brevard County, Florida, Case No 05-2006-CA-052659 granting Sandy Kaye Motion to Reset Foreclosure Sale, filed December 4, 2010

There are no [appellate] opinions below. This Court might consider some means of inducing an appeals court to render an opinion in cases of summary judgment, so draconian in its outcome, as is this case, to accommodate a more orderly appeal to the Supreme Court of the United States.

JURISDICTION

The Supreme Court of the United States has jurisdiction.

28 U.S.C. § 1254(1) The statute mandates that:

> Cases in the courts of appeals may be reviewed by the Supreme Court by the following methods:
> (1) By writ of certiorari granted upon the petition of any party to any civil or criminal case, before or after rendition of judgment or decree.

Lower court, Eighteenth Judicial District, 05-2006-CA-052659, affirmed by 5th District Court of Appeal of Florida, 5D10-98, per curiam, on January 31, 2012

Order of 5th District denying rehearing, on March 1, 2012

Appeal to Florida Supreme Court March 30, 2012 docketed as SC12-692

Florida Supreme Court disposition May 1, 2012: dismissed for lack of jurisdiction.

CONSTITUTIONAL AND STATUTORY PROVISIONS

The questions presented to the Court involve the Seventh Amendment which provides that "[i]n Suits at common law, . . . the right of trial by jury shall be preserved, and no fact tried by jury, shall be otherwise re-examined in any Court of the United States, than according to the rules of the common law."

The questions presented are also governed by the Fifth and Fourteenth Amendments (which states "nor shall any State deprive any person of life, liberty, or property, without due process of law"). The guarantee of due process mandates that all governments respect the rights and protections granted by the U.S. Constitution before that government can deprive a person of life, liberty, or property. Due process guarantees that a person will receive a fair, orderly, and just trial. While the Fifth Amendment applies to the United States government, the identical text in the Fourteenth Amendment applies this due process requirement to the states and its governments.

Due process requires " 'fair notice and a real opportunity to be heard at a meaningful time and in a meaningful manner'" to insure fair treatment when parties face 'governmental decisions that deprive individuals of liberty or property interests.' " in *Constitutional Law: Due Process* 34 Stetson L. Rev. 829 (2004-2005) Daigneault, Jay.

The summary judgment process has been abused and threatens our property, our liberty and our lives.

To take a person's home, all of his property, at a late stage in life, when he has little possibility of regaining the sum of his life's work, destroys his liberty and wrecks his life. It is the essence of tyranny. The state need not kill a man, it need only "tax" him to death, rob him of his wealth and render him powerless.

Statement of the Case

On July 31 2006 Sandy Kaye filed an invalid, hearsay, lien for $6,210.00 (Six thousand two hundred ten dollars) (record p. 58) on Thomas Jewusiak's homestead, which lien was sworn to by their attorney who was not their managing agent and had no personal knowledge of whether the amount was owed. The homestead is a two story penthouse apartment on the top floors within the Sandy Kaye apartment house, under condominium ownership.

$5,850. 00 of that lien amount of $6,210.00 was charged for "window caulking" for the permanently closed windows on the oceanfront side of Thomas Jewusiak's homestead.

Sandy Kaye singled out Thomas Jewusiak as the only unit owner to be charged a special assessment of $5,850.00, purportedly for caulking, in retaliation for his suit against the Sandy Kaye for negligence, in Sandy Kaye's failure to maintain the Sandy Kaye apartment house, thereby allowing massive amounts of water to intrude upon and damage Thomas Jewusiak's homestead, especially during the hurricanes of 2004.

The condo documents make clear Sandy Kaye's responsibility to maintain the exterior envelope, reserving only the windows that 'open', to be maintained by the individual unit owners. The windows that do not open were excluded from the responsibility of the unit owners because the 'closed windows' require a ladder or scaffolding to reach, which would require minimal effort to maintain during regular maintenance and painting of the apartment building, since the scaffolding would already be available.

Sandy Kaye chose to interpret 'open' to mean closed. Although caulking is a relatively inexpensive undertaking, Sandy Kaye chose to have the work performed from a lift, which cost 90% of the total $5,850.00 Sandy Kaye claims to have paid. Thomas Jewusiak has asserted to Sandy Kaye and subsequently swore in affidavit form that the windows did not need caulking, that Thomas Jewusiak regularly caulked his windows and that the source of water intrusion over which he was suing Sandy Kaye was caused by latent construction defects (lack of flashing around windows, cracks in the concrete block, and failure of proper maintenance by Sandy Kaye of 'cool decking' which allowed water to intrude under the doors; and lack of maintenance overall by the Sandy Kaye.)

Not only is the claim of lien an invalid hearsay document, but Sandy Kaye's original complaint (page 53 of the record) is not a verified complaint. The documents attached are not introduced by affidavit, nor are they sworn to or certified by proper authority or their foundation established.

Sandy Kaye's amended complaint (page 72) is similarly lacking, containing documents without authority, certification or foundation, including condo documents.

Sandy Kaye does not lay the foundation for the 'certificate of amendments' which it merely attaches (April 26, 2006) nor does it establish its authority to pass such an amendment without unanimous approval of Sandy Kaye condominium members, since it violates the tenor of the original declaration.

The purported article " 7.1 (6)(B)(5) amendment to the declaration 'permits the association [Sandy Kaye] to lien for work performed by the association in the event a unit owner fails to maintain their unit".

So, Sandy Kaye is alleging that Thomas Jewusiak did not caulk his windows. <u>However, Sandy Kaye never had the windows inspected, before having them caulked</u>, nor did it notify Thomas Jewusiak to caulk them.

On Jan 8, 2007 Sandy Kaye records a 'notice of filing' and merely attaches without corroborating affidavit or certification what alleges to be a 'certificate of amendments.'

On Jan 12, 2007 Sandy Kaye files its amended complaint (page 72) in much the same form as the first, no affidavit, no certification, no foundation for either business records or public records. Sandy Kaye merely attaches the same 'claim of lien' (page 78) filed July 31, 2006 which was never noticed for foreclosure. The 30 day notice of foreclosure letter, merely attached (page 83), is dated June 27, 2006, sent before the lien is filed.

On January 25, 2007 Thomas Jewusiak filed his answer and affirmative defenses (page 85) which repeat that the windows that do not open, are the maintenance responsibility of Sandy Kaye, and without filing a counter claim Thomas Jewusiak states that it is Sandy Kaye who is, in fact, negligent in maintaining the envelope of the building, stating: "Furthermore that the windows and doors were improperly installed" and are therefore a latent defect, the responsibility of Sandy Kaye to remedy. In effect, that Sandy Kaye cannot sue for negligence when they are in fact responsible to maintain the very windows (that do not open) that they allege, without any evidence presented anywhere in the record, was improperly maintained by Thomas Jewusiak.

On April 16, 2007 Sandy Kaye files its first motion for final summary judgment (page 99)

On July 31, 2007 Thomas Jewusiak files his first affidavit in opposition to motion for final summary judgment with 'personal knowledge', swearing under oath to the facts stated therein.

On May 1, 2008 Thomas Jewusiak, pro se, files his second affidavit 'in opposition to motion for final summary judgment of foreclosure'. Once again, Thomas Jewusiak repeats his previous affirmative defenses, (page 135) (page 9) clarifying:

"...that since the fixed windows are clearly the responsibility of Sandy Kaye to maintain, the caulking cost for [Jewusiak's] fixed windows should have been equally assessed to all 28 unit owners.(page 136) .....12. The Plaintiff [Sandy Kaye] has not submitted any testimony from any expert that the windows and doors did in fact need caulking,' .... (page 136) "15. Your affiant [Thomas Jewusiak] has submitted to the plaintiff an experts report from William Gibson indicating that there is some water intrusion around the fixed windows because of a construction defect, a lack of proper flashing. Such construction defects clearly become the responsibility of the condominium association, the Sandy Kaye." .... (page 136) "Plaintiff [Sandy Kaye] never notified the affiant [Thomas Jewusiak] that it intended to caulk the subject windows nor did it give the affiant [Thomas Jewusiak] the opportunity to caulk affiant's [Thomas Jewusiak]'s fixed windows, as useless as such an endeavor would have been..." (page136) "19. Caulking is an inexpensive process for which the plaintiff [Sandy Kaye] vastly overpaid. Ninety percent of the cost they paid was for the use of a 'lift' which was unnecessary. The windows and doors were recently painted by the Sandy Kaye by means of ladder and a mason's scaffold, both relatively inexpensive."

Thomas Jewusiak files his third (page 206) "affidavit in opposition to motion for final summary judgment of foreclosure." On November 3, 2008 a summary judgment trial was held by Judge Turner. Sandy Kaye's motion was denied, an order signed by the lower tribunal on November 12, 2008 (page 212)

On January 28, 2009 Thomas Jewusiak filed (page 221) a motion to demand a jury trial, four days for defendant's [Thomas Jewusiak's] allotted time for trial, and that the court allow sufficient time for discovery and leave to file a cross-claim. This motion was denied by the lower tribunal, (Appendix pg. 1-2) evidencing the court's intent to deprive Thomas Jewusiak of due process even if summary judgment was denied.

Thomas Jewusiak's third affidavit in opposition to summary judgment repeats the facts already sworn to in previous affidavits and Thomas Jewusiak further states (page 228):

" 13 The defendant was not allowed to examine the records of the Sandy Kaye condominium in violation of Florida law"... "14. All of these issues are ripe for discovery and the defendant [Jewusiak] will need to examine the records of the Sandy Kaye and to depose witnesses and submit interrogatories to plaintiff [Sandy Kaye]."

On February 16, 2009 the court allowed one -half hour to 'hear' Thomas Jewusiak's motion, all requests and the demand for jury trial were denied; order signed February 26, 2009. (record page 238) (Appendix pg. 1-2)

On March 4, 2009 mediation took place at the Melbourne office of Sandy Kaye's counsel (at 6767 North Wickham Road Suite 400, where Thomas Jewusiak delivered his motion affidavit in answer to Sandy Kaye's final motion for summary judgment), without success.

On March 11, 2009 Thomas Jewusiak filed (page 269):

'Motion to compel the Plaintiff to produce for review and copying by the defendant a current account and a monthly, bimonthly or quarterly statement of account for each unit (within the Sandy Kaye condominium) designating the name of the unit owner the due date and the amount paid upon the account and the balance due, for that unit starting with the present and working back to 2003, and that the court' grant a continuance for the purpose of the defendant examining the subject documents."

Thomas Jewusiak's motion, in detail, explains the refusal of the Sandy Kaye to allow Thomas Jewusiak to examine the records in violation of Fla.Stat. 718.111 and further states:

"The defendant [Jewusiak] is willing to subject the results of his own examination of the Sandy Kaye financial records to a Certified Public Accountant for verification. The defendant [Jewusiak] is willing and hereby proposes that the amount in controversy concerning the regular assessments be paid by the defendant into an independent escrow account until such time as the defendant is allowed to examine the subject records and determine the amount, if any, that he owes."

These regular monthly assessments are to be distinguished from the "special assessment" for which Thomas Jewusiak was singled out.

(page 286) On March 13, 2009 Thomas Jewusiak filed a motion for 'continuance because the plaintiff did not serve the defendant with notice for trial thereby depriving the defendant [Thomas Jewusiak] of the opportunity to object, that the matters are not 'at issue and ready for trial.' The lower tribunal refused to hear or consider this motion thus depriving Thomas Jewusiak of due process.

On March 13, 2009, Thomas Jewusiak filed a notice of case management conference (285) which also was ignored by Sandy Kaye and the lower tribunal.

(page 301) (page 303)

On March 17 Thomas Jewusiak filed numerous exhibits as proofs in a sworn affidavit-motion.

These affidavits were again referenced in Thomas Jewusiak's May 26 final affidavit in opposition to summary judgment, swearing 'personal knowledge':

" 3. The documents referenced as exhibits and thereby made a part here of (which are part of the court record) are true and correct copies of the originals as kept in the files of the defendant- affiant

[Jewusiak], under defendant's [Jewusiak's] continual personal custody to be used at trial."

(page 759) On May 8, 2009 Sandy Kaye filed an amended motion for final summary judgment containing only the hearsay assertions of Sandy Kaye's counsel, which is not in affidavit form. The documents are merely attached without certification or proper foundation. The only affidavit attached is for attorney's fees.

This unsworn to, hearsay, document does admit, however:

(page 761) "17... The Board of Directors never saw windows leak. However, there was evidence of water leaking into the unit below."

(page 774) On May 26, 2009 Thomas Jewusiak filed with the clerk and hand delivered to the Melbourne office of Sandy Kaye's counsel his affidavit in opposition, two days before the scheduled trial, as mandated by in FRCP (page 510).

The Sandy Kaye's motion for summary judgment does not address each of Thomas Jewusiak's affirmative defenses, most are ignored; neither does it address or counter by way of affidavit or other proofs Thomas Jewusiak's numerous affidavits that were already part of the record.

Sandy Kaye's counsel, by hearsay, in its motion for summary judgment attempts to define 'open' to include the permanently closed windows:

"Included within the responsibility of the apartment owner shall be windows, screens and doors opening into or onto his apartment."

The first definition Sandy Kaye quotes for open: " '1. (A) Affording unobstructed entrance and exit, not shut or closed'." This first definition, in fact, proves the case against Sandy Kaye's interpretation of the word open.

Sandy Kaye does not explain on what basis it is resubmitting a motion for summary judgment given the fact that its previous motion was denied by Judge Turner; no error or fraud is alleged nor are any circumstances of the case alleged to have changed; nor does Sandy Kaye even mention in its new motion for summary judgment that a previous Judge had denied summary judgment.

Sandy Kaye's newest motion lacks proofs and does not contain '… any affidavits, answers to interrogatories, admissions, depositions and other materials' nor does it make reference to any "proof" that is part of the court record.

Sandy Kaye failed to state in its motions with particularity the grounds upon which it is based and the substantial matters of law to be argued.

The lower tribunal refused to accept as timely Thomas Jewusiak's final motion affidavit in opposition; Sandy Kaye had ignored it, failing thus to counter the proofs referenced therein.

However, all of the proofs were already in the "record" and all of the affirmative defenses had been enumerated in previous affidavits in opposition to summary judgment:

1. That the permanently closed windows are the maintenance responsibility of Sandy Kaye.
2. That Sandy Kay offers no evidence, expert or otherwise, that the windows needed caulking; Sandy Kaye never examined the windows.
3. That the windows have a latent defect, a lack of proper flashing and thus, if not already, became the responsibility of Sandy Kaye .
4. That Thomas Jewusiak was never notified to caulk the permanently closed windows.
5. That Thomas Jewusiak regularly caulked his windows and doors.
6. That the actual sources of water intrusion, enumerated in great detail in Thomas Jewusiak's affidavits, are the chimney, skylights, roof, failure of cool decking (under doors) and are the result of negligence of Sandy Kaye.
7. That Thomas Jewusiak has not been permitted to examine the books of the Sandy Kaye in an orderly or proper manner.

8. That Thomas Jewusiak offered to deposit the regular monthly assessment into an escrow account or the court registry until allowed to examine Sandy Kaye records.

The lower tribunal allowed only one hour for the summary judgment trial. (Thomas Jewusiak requested four days to present his case to a jury.)

The lower tribunal by its' own admission was unfamiliar with the record and did not examine it as required, admitting that it did not read the entire affidavit in opposition.

(26) Concerning the affidavit of May 26, 2009: "The Court : I obviously, did not have the chance to read it all."

The lower tribunal abused judicial discretion by disallowing Thomas Jewusiak's affidavit in opposition because the affidavit was hand delivered 2 days before the trial to the Melbourne office of Sandy Kaye's counsel and not counsel's Maitland office.

The lower tribunal did not address all of the numerous defenses presented by Thomas Jewusiak in previous motions in opposition and in the proofs in the record.

The lower tribunal took testimony from Sandy Kaye's counsel at the hearing and weighed facts based on counsel's testimony; counsel did not argue but rather testified on the basis of what could only be hearsay since Sandy Kaye had no proofs in record.

The lower tribunal did acknowledge some of the material issues: (page 33) **"The Court: ... and a caulking may be a temporary fix to the problem. But if the proper flashing is not there, it is just a temporary fix and there may be future water intrusion whether it's just wear and tear or future hurricanes."**

(page 33) **"The Court: The flashing itself is not part of the window unit.**

Ms. Kirtland: Correct. [Kirtland testifying as "expert", which she is not.]

The Court: That's put in during original construction and never changed as part of regular maintenance unless there is a defect."

(page 45) [Thomas Jewusiak]: "These have all been addressed by experts, and the plaintiff, Sandy Kaye, and Ms. Kirkland do not have one single expert witness testimony report. They are simply talking off the cuff...."

(page 43) "Mr. Jewusiak: ... Just that I think that the main fact that this motion is so deficient, that it includes no proofs, no affidavits of any kind, no references to the record of any affidavits, depositions or expert testimony."

(page 44) Sandy Kaye's counsel asserts that this is a contract case. It is not. It is a negligence case based upon an erroneous reading of a, perhaps, slightly ambiguous contract, turning on the ordinary meaning of the word "open".

(page 48) "The Court: There are lots of affidavits and other supporting documentation in the file from both sides to support the positions of both sides."

The lower tribunal is wrong. There are no substantive affidavits or proofs on the record for Sandy Kaye. Even if this were the case, it would indicate that there are material facts at issue and therefore summary judgment would be inappropriate.

The lower tribunal addresses only a few of Thomas Jewusiak's affirmative defenses.

(page 48-49) The lower tribunal in its summary judgment order, (Appendix pg. 3-17) in effect, defines closed to mean open and finds Thomas Jewusiak responsible for the maintenance of the fixed windows, by weighing hearsay allegations of Sandy Kaye's counsel and determines that these windows required caulking.

Thomas Jewusiak's affidavit in opposition was, in fact, properly served in person two days before the hearing; filed with the clerk and personally accepted by someone claiming to represent the Sandy Kaye's counsel at their Melbourne office.

(page 859) The lower tribunal's order granting summary judgment, (Appendix pg. 3-17) does not address each of the affirmative defenses raised by Thomas Jewusiak.

Thomas Jewusiak filed a motion with lower tribunal to cancel the foreclosure sale, citing a Florida case, *Fisher v. Tanglewood* (page 888) (5th DCA 1996), wherein the condominium association (plaintiffs) action against the defendant for foreclosure of a lien securing assessment, issues of material fact existed as to the validity of the assessments, precluding summary judgment.

(page 970-980) Thomas Jewusiak files notice of appeal to and is finally able to raise the filing fee. The Fifth District Court of Appeals of Florida acknowledges a new case on Jan 14, 2010, (page 981)

On April 1, 2010 Thomas Jewusiak files with the lower tribunal an affidavit-motion (which the lower tribunal refused to hear)(page 996-1008); asking that the pending foreclosure sale be cancelled because the original claim of lien is an invalid hearsay document, swearing to matters of which the affiant, the counsel to Sandy Kaye, has no personal knowledge.

This affidavit of Thomas Jewusiak also outlines (page 1043) the tortious interference of Sandy Kaye in sabotaging an impending sale of Thomas Jewusiak's homestead.

On May 11, 2011 Thomas Jewusiak filed a motion objecting to the special terms of the sale dictated by the "Third Final Judgment of Foreclosure". This motion outlines the onerous terms designed to favor Sandy Kaye over all other bidders. None of these special terms are revealed in the notice of sale published by Sandy Kaye. (page 1048-1049)

On May 18, 2010 (page 1106) Thomas Jewusiak filed with the lower tribunal clerk a motion requesting that the lower tribunal direct the clerk to accept a supersedeas bond which the clerk told Thomas Jewusiak she would not accept, after previously telling him she would accept it.

On May 19 2010 at 10:44 AM Thomas Jewusiak filed with the clerk of the lower tribunal "Notice…whereby the defendant deposits cash with the clerk of the court as bond to stay the foreclosure sale on defendant's homestead". After receiving directions from the lower tribunal by phone the lower tribunal clerk would not accept the cash as bond.

On May 19, 2010 Thomas Jewusiak tenders payment to the clerk of the lower tribunal of the full judgment amount. The clerk refuses to accept this payment insisting that "arrangements" must be made directly with Sandy Kaye.

On May 20 Thomas Jewusiak filed an affidavit motion requesting that the lower tribunal vacate the foreclosure sale. The motion was not an objection to the sale price. The lower tribunal heard this motion telephonically by ambush. Thomas Jewusiak picked up his phone and was told by the judicial assistant that Judge Roberts would be on the line along with counsel for Sandy Kaye. The 'hearing', if it can be called that, was extremely brief; motion denied (page 1169) Thomas Jewusiak was again denied due process, denied proper notice to prepare and to be heard.

On June 1, 2010 (page1133-1168) Thomas Jewusiak filed his objection to sale based on price. The lower tribunal refused to hear this motion claiming, contrary to fact, that it had heard the objection to sale in the previous motion of May 20, 2010, stating in its order of June 7, 2010 (1171): "This objection is denied since the court previously heard same on May 24, 2010." This is incorrect.

The lower tribunal further states in its order of denial: "Thomas Jewusiak is barred from filing any more objections to this sale." This is a violation of Thomas Jewusiak's constitutional due process right to be heard duly raised. This objection to sale based on price was denied without hearing.

Arguments

(1) Sandy Kaye's original claim of lien was a document based on the hearsay allegations of their attorney, who was not their agent, in the management of the Sandy Kaye apartment house, and was not the custodian of their business records and had no personal

knowledge of the subject to which she testified; she was their attorney, only.

(2) Sandy Kaye's Final Motion for Summary Judgment includes no proofs nor does it reference any proofs in the record. Sandy Kaye's "affidavits", as few as there are, are not competent evidence and do not meet the requirements to support summary judgment.

(3) Sandy Kaye does not counter or disprove any of Thomas Jewusiak's affirmative defenses or affidavits (all of which were in the record when Sandy Kaye filed its final Motion for Summary judgment) by proper affidavit of its own or by other competent evidence. It is well established that summary final judgment is appropriate only where each affirmative defense has been conclusively refuted on the record.

(4) Simply attaching a document to a motion or pleading, as Sandy Kaye does, does not make it proof. Its' foundation must be established. The lower tribunal should have excluded from consideration, on a motion for summary judgment, any document that is not a certified attachment to a proper affidavit.

(5) Without any proofs, or competent evidence by way of affidavit or certified attachments to a proper affidavit, in the record, Sandy Kaye should not have been granted summary judgment.

(6) Sandy Kaye did not establish the validity of any of their assessments. Where the validity of assessments remains a contested issue, summary judgment must not be granted.

(7) Sandy Kaye's affidavit of indebtedness, in and of itself, is not sufficient competent evidence. Sandy Kaye failed to factually and conclusively refute Thomas Jewusiak's affirmative defenses on the record.
The affidavit of indebtedness by itself does not disprove the affirmative defenses raised by Thomas Jewusiak and failed to demonstrate the legal insufficiency of those defenses.

(8) Contract Ambiguity: The lower tribunal improperly and erroneously interpreted a contract, the condominium covenants between Sandy Kaye and Thomas Jewusiak. The lower tribunal could not have concluded (weighed the facts) that Thomas Jewusiak was responsible for caulking the permanently closed windows unless it interpreted this contract, and defined the word 'open' to mean closed, thus to include the permanently closed windows that are the subject of this controversy. If this contract is ambiguous, with the possibility that open can mean closed, then it a question of fact, to be determined by a trier of fact and inappropriate for summary judgment.

We need not run to dictionaries, nor are we required or even allowed to do so; words must be given their ordinary, obvious meanings as commonly understood:
"Due regard must be had for the purpose contemplated by the parties to the covenant, and words used must be given their ordinary, obvious meaning as commonly understood at the time the instrument containing the covenants was executed...." (MOORE'S FED. PRACTICE, 106 So. at 903). "Any doubt as to the meaning of the words used must be resolved against those seeking enforcement."

(9) Weighed Facts: The lower tribunal conducted a trial, hearing testimony, hearsay testimony from Sandy Kaye's counsel and came to conclusions of fact based on that hearsay "evidence" (Appendix pg. 3-17): that Thomas Jewusiak was responsible for caulking the permanently closed windows, that he did not caulk them, that they needed caulking, that Thomas Jewusiak was notified that they needed caulking, that these "closed" windows did in fact leak, that Sandy Kaye paid $5850 for this caulking; all on the hearsay testimony of Sandy Kaye's counsel with no other competent evidence in the record to support it.

In a summary judgment the lower tribunal is not permitted to weigh the facts or reach conclusions concerning them because by so doing it would be depriving the litigant [Thomas Jewusiak] of a jury trial which he had demanded. In summary judgment it is well-established that the court may neither adjudge the credibility of the witnesses nor weigh the evidence, nor may the trial court determine factual issues; but it is only allowed to determine whether a genuine issue of material fact exists.

However, in the case at hand, the lower tribunal did not weigh the facts, there were no facts from Sandy Kaye to weigh, rather it took the hearsay allegations of Sandy Kaye's counsel as fact and made determinations of fact based upon it and ruled accordingly. (Appendix pg. 3-17)

(10) In summary judgment Thomas Jewusiak was not required to prove his case with clear and convincing evidence but merely to show that a material fact was in dispute, which he did.

(11) Denial of Trial by Jury (Appendix pg. 1-2): Even before the truncated summary judgment trial, the lower tribunal violated Thomas Jewusiak's constitutional rights when it refused him even the possibility of the right to a trial by jury.

Also, by refusing to allow Thomas Jewusiak the four days necessary to present his case, by refusing to allow Thomas Jewusiak to file any additional motions, the lower tribunal deprived him of due process: due process a real opportunity to be heard "at a meaningful time and in a meaningful manner" to insure fair treatment when individuals face governmental decisions that deprive them of their life, liberty or property.

(12) Sandy Kaye does produce one suspect, so-called Affidavit of Indebtedness. (by Keith Johnson) (Supplement to the Record Vol 1): the original document is missing; no certified true copy stamped by the lower tribunal clerk is in possession of Sandy Kaye nor could such a certified true copy be produced by Sandy Kaye; (the affidavit was not sent up to the 5th District Court of Appeal when Thomas Jewusiak ordered the entire record); it was never received by Jewusiak; a copy was accepted by the 5th District Court of Appeal to supplement the record (without any affidavit or other authentication from the lower tribunal clerk as to how this copy was made, why we should accept it as legitimate in place of the missing original and what exactly did happen to the original); out there all by itself in a kind of limbo; unreferenced in the complaint; unreferenced and unattached to the motion for summary judgment; it is a statement of purported ultimate fact, conclusory, and therefore unable to support summary judgment; such documents are admissible only if the affidavit specifically cites the facts which

justify the conclusion and yet Sandy Kaye fights tooth and nail to submit this ineffectual copy, their only affidavit of note, pretending to be evidence. It cannot be said to "verify" the complaint, after the fact. It is apodictic, self-evident on its face; one needs no legal scholar to run to the law library to conclude that such "it's all true" affidavits are the equivalent of legal rubbish.

PROOF OF THE ARGUMENTS

It is appropriate for a court to grant summary judgment only if the discovery materials, and any affidavits before the Court show that there is no genuine issue as to any material fact and that the movant is entitled to judgment as a matter of law. See Fed.R.Civ.P. 56(c) "[A] party seeking summary judgment always bears the initial responsibility of informing the . . . court of the basis for its motion, and . . . [must] demonstrate the absence of a genuine issue of material fact." *Celotex Corp. v. Catrett*, 477 U.S. 317, 323, 106 S.Ct. 2548, 91 L.Ed.2d 265 (1986). Courts must review the evidentiary materials submitted in support of a motion for summary judgment to ensure that the motion is supported by evidence. If the evidence submitted in support of the summary judgment motion does not meet the movant's burden, then summary judgment must be denied. Hearsay evidence cannot be considered on a motion for summary judgment. *Wiley v. United*

States, 20 F.3d 222, 226 (6th Cir. 1994). Any documentary evidence submitted in support of summary judgment must either be properly authenticated or self authenticating under the Federal Rules of Evidence. *Goguen v. Textron, Inc.*, 234 F.R.D. 13, 16 (D. Mass. 2006). The movant's statement of material facts as to which the movant contends no genuine fact exists must refer with particularity to those proofs in the record upon which the movant relies. Sandy Kaye submitted no proofs.

Major League Baseball Props. v. Salvino, Inc., 542 F.3d 290, 310 (2d Cir. 2008) ("'[H]earsay testimony . . . that would not be admissible if testified to at the trial may not properly be set forth in [the Rule 56(e)] affidavit.'") (quoting *Beyah v. Coughlin*, 789 F.2d 986, 989 (2d Cir. 1986) (quoting 6 MOORE'S FED. PRACTICE ¶ 56.22[1], at 56-1312 to 56-1316 (2d ed. 1985))); *Jenkins v. Winter*, 540 F.3d 742, 748 (8th Cir. 2008)

United States v. $92,203.00 in U.S. Currency, 537 F.3d 504, 508 (5th Cir. 2008) (finding that the district court erred by not striking the affidavit used to support summary judgment because "the affidavit clearly contained hearsay, was not based on personal knowledge, and, under normal summary judgment procedures, is not admissible") (citing *Bolen v. Dengel*, 340 F.3d 300, 313 (5th Cir. 2003); FED. R.CIV. P. 56(e)(1)); *Ward v. Int'l Paper Co.*, 509 F.3d 457, 462 (8th Cir. 2007) (declining to consider affidavits containing inadmissible hearsay on summary judgment because "nothing in the affidavits indicates a hearsay exception applies"); *Alpert v. United States*, 481 F.3d 404, 409 (6th Cir. 2007)

Argo v. Blue Cross & Blue Shield of Kan., Inc., 452 F.3d 1193, 1199 (10th Cir.2006) ("The requirement that the substance of the evidence must be admissible is not only explicit in Rule 56, which provides that '[s]upporting and opposing affidavits shall . . . set forth such facts as would be admissible in evidence,' FED. R.CIV. P. 56(e), but also implicit in the court's role at the summary judgment stage. *Argo* explains: "Thus, for example, at summary judgment courts should disregard inadmissible hearsay statements *contained* in affidavits, as those statements could not be presented at trial in any form." *Id.* (citing *Hardy v. S.F. Phosphates Ltd. Co.*, 185 F.3d 1076, 1082 n.5 (10th Cir.1999)).

Macuba v. Deboer, 193 F. 3d 1316 - Court of Appeals, 11th Circuit 1999: concluded that an affidavit containing hearsay could not be considered on summary judgment because the hearsay statements were being offered for their truth, none of the statements would be admissible at trial under an exception to the hearsay rule.

Bradley Scott Shannon argues: "Federal Rule of Civil Procedure 56 is best interpreted as imposing a strict standard with respect to the admissibility of materials presented by parties at summary judgment, a standard that approximates a party's evidentiary burden at trial."

Anderson v. United States, 417 U.S. 211,219 & n.7 (1974); Duane, *supra* note 198, at 1532: indicates that the burden of evidence is lighter for the non-movant in summary judgment. Hearsay is defined as an out-of-court statement offered for the truth of the matter asserted. Materials offered in opposition to summary judgment, however, are not offered to establish the truth of the matter asserted. They are offered to establish that a genuine issue of material fact exists for trial. The non-movant is not required to prove his case but only to establish that a material fact is in controversy.

In William W. Schwarzer, Alan Hirsch & David J. Barrans, *The Analysis & Decision of Summary Judgment Motions: A Monograph on Rule 56 of the Federal Rules of Civil Procedure*, 139 F.R.D. 441, 481 (1992), the authors argue that *Celotex* clarifies the nonmovant's right to oppose a summary judgment motion with any of the materials listed in Rule 14.

Anderson v. Liberty Lobby, Inc., the Supreme Court stated that a judge ruling upon a summary judgment motion "is not himself to weigh the evidence and determine the truth of the matter" involved in the litigation.

James Joseph Duane notes that the statement from *Celotex* indicating that "a nonmovant is not required to 'produce evidence in a form that would be admissible at trial in order to avoid summary judgment,'" *id.*, did not override the apparent requirement in Rule 56(e) that all supporting and opposing affidavits set forth facts that would be admissible in evidence," *id.* Duane states:

> "I respectfully submit that Justice Rehnquist's statement can be understood far better by reading it with the emphasis supplied elsewhere, to say that the nonmoving party is not required to "produce evidence in a form that would be admissible at trial in order to avoid summary judgment"—but without altering in any way Rule 56(e)'s requirement that the affidavit be admissible, both in content and form, at the summary judgment stage, where the court is deciding an altogether different question. As we have seen, where an affidavit is being considered on a summary judgment motion and is based on the personal knowledge of the affiant, it is not hearsay at all, either in content or form, even though the same affidavit will be hearsay if it is later offered at trial to prove the truth of the events described in the affidavit."

Even if Sandy Kaye had submitted proofs, which it did not, all inferences should have been drawn in favor of Thomas Jewusiak. In evaluating a summary judgment motion, the court must draw all reasonable inferences in favor of the non-moving party. *Matsushita Elec. Indus. Co. v. Zenith Radio Corp.*,

475 U.S. 574, 587, 106 S.Ct. 1348, 89 L.Ed.2d 538 (1986).

Conclusory statements in affidavits should be disregarded. To support a conclusory statement it is necessary to include sufficient factual information in the affidavit and to establish that the conclusion is in fact based on personal knowledge and that the witness is in fact competent to so testify, even when the affiant states that the affidavit is made on personal knowledge. (FEDERAL RULES OF EVIDENCE)

If the evidence raises any issue of material fact, if it is conflicting, if it will permit different reasonable inferences, or if it tends to prove the issues, it should be submitted to the jury as a question of fact to be determined by that jury.

Conclusion

The Court should grant this petition for the reasons stated herein.

Respectfully Submitted by Thomas G. Jewusiak

May 30, 2012

Revised July 31, 2012

IN THE CIRCUIT COURT, OF THE EIGHTEENTH JUDICIAL CIRCUIT, IN AND FOR BREVARD COUNTY, FLORIDA
CASE NO 05-2006-CA-052659
GENERAL JURISDICTION DIVISION

SANDY KAYE CONDOMINIUM ASSOCIATION, INC, a Florida not for profit corporation

Plaintiff,

v

THOMAS JEWUSIAK and UNKNOWN SPOUSE OF THOMAS JEWUSIAK,

Defendants

ORDER

THIS MATTER having been heard in Court on February 16, 2009, and after hearing arguments of counsel for the Plaintiff and arguments from Thomas Jewusiak, Pro Se Defendant, it is hereby

ORDERED AND ADJUDGED

1   Defendant's demand for Jury Trial is hereby denied.

2   Defendant's request for Continuance is hereby denied and all discovery has to be done as set forth in the trial order.

3   Defendant's request for a counter-claim is hereby denied.

4   Depending on the issues at trial, the Court will determine whether or not the trial needs to be more than one day which was allotted in the trial order.

DONE AND ORDERED in Chambers at Brevard County, Florida, on this 26 day of February, 2009

s/ David Dugan

HONORABLE DAVID DUGAN
CIRCUIT COURT JUDGE

Copies furnished to
Thomas Jewusiak
Marlene L Kirtland, Esq.

IN THE CIRCUIT COURT, OF THE
EIGHTEENTH JUDICIAL CIRCUIT, IN AND
FOR BREVARD COUNTY, FLORIDA
CASE NO 05-2006-CA-052659
GENERAL JURISDICTION DIVISION

SANDY KAYE CONDOMINIUM ASSOCIATION,
INC , a Florida not-for profit corporation,
Plaintiff

v

THOMAS JEWUSIAK and UNKNOWN SPOUSE
OF THOMAS JEWUSIAK,

Defendants   Publish in Brevard Reporter

FINAL SUMMARY JUDGMENT

THIS CAUSE having come before the Court on Plaintiff's Motion for Final Summary Judgment of Foreclosure and Award of Attorney's Fees and Costs, the Court having considered the pleadings and proofs submitted, including Plaintiffs Affidavit of Costs, the detailed time records of Plaintiff's counsel, counsel's fee arrangement with Plaintiff and the guidelines established by the Supreme Court in Standard Guarantee Insurance Co v Quanstrom 555 So 2d 828 (Fla 1990) and Florida Patient's Compensation Fund v Rowe 472 So 2d 1145 (Fla 1985), having reviewed the Court file, and being otherwise duly advised in the premises,

THIS COURT finds Plaintiff's counsel has reasonably expended __55__ hours on this litigation, and that a reasonable hourly rate for the services of Plaintiff's counsel is 165 00 -200 00, yielding a lodestar which is subject neither to enhancement for the contingency risk factor, nor to reduction based on the results obtained.

This Court hereby finds that

1) The Defendant failed to properly maintain the windows in his unit in accordance with the Declaration. The Plaintiff hence properly passed the Special Assessment for caulking of the same. Defendant failed to pay the Special Assessment in the amount of $5,850 00, which is currently due.

2) The Defendant failed to pay his regular monthly assessment as required under the Declaration and 718 116 which has a current balance as of June 1, 2009 in the amount of $8954 64 A true and correct copy of the breakdown of assessments and payments is attached to this Order as Exhibit "A"

3) The Court finds that the claims of water intrusion are not part of this instant case and will not rule on the same.

4) The Court finds that the Affidavit in Opposition to Plaintiffs Motion for Summary Judgment was untimely filed.

Accordingly, it is

ORDERED AND ADJUDGED as follows:

1 This Court has jurisdiction of the subject matter hereto and the parties hereto. The equities of this cause are with the Plaintiff. There is due to the Plaintiff the sum of money as hereinafter set forth

a	Special Assessment for caulking and regular monthly assessments through 06/1/09	$25,070 00
b	Other charges through 07/11/09	00
c	Interest through 07/11/09 on said principal	2,606 83
d	Record fees/Copies/Mail/Deed Search	31 92
e	Brevard County Filing Fee	265 00
f	Title Print	60 00
g	Service of Process	72 00
	Total Costs	428 92
	Less Payments received	<u>12,720 00</u>
	SUB-TOTAL	$15,385 75
	Attorney's fees	9629 80
	TOTAL	$25,015 55

A pg. 5

2   Plaintiff holds a lien for the total sum specified in paragraph 1, plus interest at the rate of 6%, superior to any claim or estate of the Defendants upon the following described property in Brevard County, Florida:

> Unit 901, SANDY KAYE CONDOMINIUM, according to the Declaration thereof, recorded in Official Records Book 2704, Pages 0181 through 0238, inclusive. Public Records of Brevard County, Florida. Together with an undivided interest in the common elements Together with Garage Space 901, inside and exterior, as shown on the Sandy Kaye Condominium As-Built Site Plan, revised October 21, 1987, as recorded in O R. Book 2858, Pages 1106-1110, Public Records of Brevard County, Florida With the following street address 2835 Highway A1A North, Unit 901, Indialantic, Florida 32903

3   If the total sum with interest at the rate described in paragraph 2 and all costs accrued subsequent to this Judgment are not paid within five (5) days, the Clerk of this Court shall sell that property at public sale on the 15 [Hand Written] day of July , [Hand Written] 2009 to the highest bidder or bidders for cash, except as prescribed in paragraph 4, at 400 South Street, Titusville, Florida 32780,

A pg. 6

in 1st Floor at 11 00 a m, in accordance with Section 45 031, Florida Statutes The Clerk of the Court shall not conduct said sale unless Plaintiff or Plaintiffs representative is present

4 Plaintiff shall advance all subsequent costs of this action and shall be reimbursed for them by the Clerk if Plaintiff is not the purchaser of the property for sale If Plaintiff is the purchaser, the Clerk shall credit Plaintiffs bid with the total sum with interest and cost accruing subsequent to this judgment, or such part of it, as is necessary to pay the bid in full

5 On filing the Certificate of Title the Clerk shall distribute the proceeds of the sale, so far as they are sufficient by paying first, all of the Plaintiffs costs, second, Plaintiffs attorneys' fees, third, the total sum due to Plaintiff, less the items paid, plus interest at the rate prescribed in paragraph 2 from this date to the date of the sale, and by retaining any remaining amount pending the further order of this Court The purchaser of the sale shall pay the documentary stamps m accordance with Florida law

6 In accordance with Section 45 0315, Florida Statutes, upon the Clerk filing the Certificate of Sale, Defendants shall forever be barred and foreclosed of any and all equity or right of redemption in and to the property Subsequently, upon the Clerk filing the Certificate of Title, the sale

shall stand confirmed and Defendants and all persons claiming an interest in the property since the filing of the Notice of Lis Pendens, shall be foreclosed of all other estate or claim in the property, and the purchaser at the sale shall be let into possession of the property, and the Clerk shall issue a Writ of Possession upon the request of said purchaser, his representatives or assigns, without further order of this Court

      7   Jurisdiction over the subject matter and the parties hereto is reserved for the purpose of entering such further orders and judgments as are necessary and proper, including but not limited to, orders and judgments for a deficiency and orders and judgments providing for the extinguishment of any other interest in the subject property subordinate to Plaintiffs interest therein

      8. Required by F.S. §45.021 and §45.032: If this property is sold at public auction, there may be additional money from the sale after payment of persons who are entitled to be paid from the sale proceeds pursuant to this final judgment.

      a.   If you are a subordinate lienholder claiming a right to funds remaining after the sale, you must file a claim with the clerk no later than 60 days after the sale. If you fail to file a claim, you will not be entitled to any remaining funds.

      b.   If the subject property has qualified for the homestead tax exemption in the most recent approved real property tax roll, please note the following:

    1.   If you are the property owner, you may claim these funds yourself. You are not required to have a lawyer or any other representation and you do not have to assign your rights to anyone else in order for you to claim any money to which you are entitled. Please check with the clerk of the court within ten (10) days after the sale to see if there is additional money from the foreclosure sale that the clerk has in registry of the court.

    2.   If you decide to sell your home or hire someone to help you claim the additional money, you should read very carefully all papers you are required to sign, ask someone else, preferably an attorney who is not related to the person offering to help you, to make sure that you understand what you are signing and that you are not transferring your property or the equity in your property without the proper information. If you cannot afford to pay an attorney, you may contact the local or nearest Legal Aid office to see if you qualify financially for their services. If they cannot assist you, they may be able to refer you to a local bar referral agency or suggest other option. If you choose to contact Legal Aid for assistance, you should do so as soon as possible after receipt of this notice.

DONE AND ORDERED in Chambers, at Brevard County, Florida, this 10 [Hand Written] day of June___[Hand Written]

        s/ David Dugan?___ [Signature Illegible]
        CIRCUIT COURT JUDGE

Plaintiff

Sandy Kaye Condominium Association, Inc
2835 Highway A1A North, Suite 101
Indialantic, FL, 32903

Defendants

Thomas Jewusiak, SSN_____
2835 Highway A1A North, Unit 901
Indialantic, FL, 32903

Copies furnished to

Sandy Kaye Condominium Association, Inc
Thomas Jewusiak

SANDY KAYE CONDOMINIUM ASSOCIATION, INC

v

THOMAS JEWUSIAK, ET AL
CASE NO 2006-CA-052659

901

Total Assessments	25070 00
Total Interest	2606 83
Total Other	0 00
Total Payments	12720 00
Balance	14956 83

Interest 10%   Per diem $ 3 80

Date	Description	Amount	Interest	Balance
	Starting balance	0 00	0 00	
5/18/2006	Special Assessment (Window Caulkin	5850 00		
6/1/2006	Maintenance	360 00	22 44	6232 44
6/30/2006	Check No 783	-720 00	49 34	5561 78
7/1/2006	Maintenance	360 00	1 52	5923 30
8/1/2006	Maintenance	360 00	50 29	6333 60
8/24/2006	Check No 792	-720 00	39 58	5653 18

A pg. 11

Date	Description	Amount	Interest
9/1/2006	Maintenance	360 00	12 39
	6025 57		
10/1/2006	Maintenance	360 00	49 42
	6434 99		
11/1/2006	Maintenance	360 00	54 13
	6849 12		
11/1/2006	Check No 809	-720 00	0 00
	6129 12		
12/1/2006	Maintenance	360 00	50 38
	6539 50		
1/1/2007	Maintenance	400 00	55 11
	6994 61		
1/3/2007	Check No 830	-760 00	3 77
	6238 39		
2/1/2007	Maintenance	400 00	49 57
	6687 95		
2/27/2007	Check No 857	-800 00	47 29
	5935 24		
3/1/2007	Maintenance	400 00	3 25
	6338 49		
3/31/2007	Special Assessment Hurricane Shutte	1500 00	52 07
	7890 56		
4/1/2007	Payment (Hurricane Shutters)		

A pg. 12

			-1500 00	2 15
	6392 71			
4/1/2007	Maintenance		400 00	0 00
	6792 71			
5/1/2007	Maintenance		400 00	55 83
	7248 54			
5/3/2007	Check No 897		-800 00	3 94
	6452 48			
6/1/2007	Maintenance		400 00	51 27
	6903 75			
7/1/2007	Maintenance		400 00	56 32
	7360 07			
7/3/2007	Check No 954		-400 00	3 97
	6964 04			
8/1/2007	Maintenance		400 00	55 33
	7419 37			
8/8/2007	Check No 973		-400 00	14 12
	7033 50			
8/9/2007	Check No 967		-400 00	1 93
	6635 42			
9/1/2007	Maintenance		400 00	41 81
	7077 24			
10/1/2007	Check No 1004		-400 00	57 83
	6735 06			

10/1/2007	Maintenance	400 00	0 00
	7135 06		
11/1/2007	Maintenance	400 00	60 60
	7595 66		
11/1/2007	Check No 1033	-400 00	0 00
	7195 66		
11/27/2007	Check No 1061	-400 00	51 26
	6846 92		
12/1/2007	Maintenance	400 00	7 50
	7254 42		

SANDY KAYE CONDOMINIUM ASSOCIATION, INC

v

THOMAS JEWUSIAK, ET AL
CASE NO 2006-CA-052659

Date	Description	Amount	Interest
	Balance		
1/1/2008	Maintenance	500 00	61 55
	7815 97		
1/3/2008	Check No 1095	-400 00	4 24
	7420 21		
1/5/2008	Check No 1096	-500 00	4 07
	6924 28		
2/1/2008	Maintenance	500 00	51 22
	7475 50		
3/1/2008	Maintenance	500 00	58 99
	8034 49		
3/6/2008	Check No 1166	-500 00	10 86
	7545 34		
3/24/2008	Check No 1183	-500 00	37 21
	7082 55		
3/31/2008	Special Assessment - Balcony Railing		
		1400 00	13 58
	8496 14		
4/1/2008	Maintenance	500 00	2 32
	8998 46		
4/29/2008	Check No 1219	-1400 00	68 91
	7667 37		

Date	Description	Amount	Balance
4/29/2008	Check No 7167 37	-500 00	0 00
5/1/2008	Maintenance 7671 29	500 00	3 93
6/1/2008	Maintenance 8236 41	500 00	65 12
7/1/2008	Maintenance 8803 54	500 00	67 13
8/1/2008	Maintenance 9377 16	500 00	73 61
8/5/2008	Payment 8887 20	-500 00	10 05
9/1/2008	Maintenance 9452 94	500 00	65 74
10/1/2008	Maintenance 10030 10	500 00	77 16
11/1/2008	Maintenance 10614 07	500 00	83 97
12/1/2008	Maintenance 11199 45	500 00	85 37
1/1/2009	Maintenance 11791 91	500 00	92 47
2/1/2009	Maintenance 12388 63	500 00	96 71

3/1/2009   Maintenance   500 00   91 19
    12979 82

4/1/2009   Maintenance   500 00   105 21
    13585 02

5/1/2009   Maintenance   500 00   105 92
    14190 95

6/1/2009   Maintenance   500 00   11370
    14804 64

7/11/2009   152 19
    14956 83

A pg. 17

IN THE CIRCUIT COURT, OF THE
EIGHTEENTH JUDICIAL CIRCUIT,
IN AND FOR BREVARD COUNTY,
FLORIDA

CASE NO 05-2006-CA-052659

GENERAL JURISDICTION DIVISION

SANDY KAYE CONDOMINIUM ASSOCIATION, INC , a Florida not for profit corporation

Plaintiff,

v

THOMAS JEWUSIAK and UNKNOWN SPOUSE OF THOMAS JEWUSIAK,

Defendants

ORDER ON MOTION TO RESET FORECLOSURE SALE

THIS CAUSE having come before the Court pursuant to Plaintiffs Motion to Reschedule The Foreclosure Sale, and the Court having reviewed the file and being otherwise advised in the premises, it is hereby

ORDERED AND ADJUDGED as follows

1 Plaintiff's Motion to re-schedule the Foreclosure Sale is Granted

2 If the total sum due with interest at the rate described in The Final Summary Judgment and all costs accrued subsequent to The Final Summary Judgment are not paid within five (5) days, the Clerk of this Court shall sell that property at public sale on

A pg. 19

SEP 30 2009 [RUBBER STAMP] 2009, to the highest bidder or bidders for cash, at Brevard County Government Center-North 518 South Palm Avenue, Brevard Room Titusville, Florida 32796 at 11 00 am, in accordance with Section 45 031, Florida Statutes The Clerk of the Court shall not conduct said sale unless Plaintiff or Plaintiffs representative is present

DONE AND ORDERED in Chambers, at Brevard County, Florida, this 17 [Hand Written] day of August [Hand Written] 2009

    s/ David Dugan [Signature Illegible, presumably that of Judge David Dugan, although not identified as such]
    CIRCUIT COURT JUDGE

Copies to

Marlene L Kirtland, Esq
Becker & Poliakoff, P A
2500 Maitland Center Parkway, #209
Maitland, Florida 32751

Thomas Jewusiak
2835 Highway A1A North, Unit 901
Indialantic, FL 32903

IN THE CIRCUIT COURT, OF THE EIGHTEENTH JUDICIAL CIRCUIT, IN AND FOR BREVARD COUNTY, FLORIDA
CASE NO. 05-2006-CA-052659   GENERAL JURISDICTION DIVISION

SANDY KAYE CONDOMINIUM ASSOCIATION, INC., a Florida not for profit corporation

Plaintiff,

v.

THOMAS JEWUSIAK and UNKNOWN SPOUSE OF THOMAS JEWUSIAK,

Defendants.   CLOSED [Rubber Stamp]

ORDER ON MOTION TO RESET FORECLOSURE SALE

THIS CAUSE having come before the Court pursuant to Plaintiffs Motion to Reschedule The Foreclosure Sale, and the Court having reviewed the file and being otherwise advised in the premises, it is hereby

ORDERED AND ADJUDGED as follows:

1. Plaintiff's Motion to re-schedule the Foreclosure Sale is Granted.

2. If the total sum due with interest at the rate described in the Amended Final Summary Judgment and all costs accrued subsequent to the Amended Final Summary Judgment are not paid within five (5) days, the Clerk of this Court shall sell that property at public sale on the Feb 3 [Hand Written], 2010, to the highest bidder or bidders for cash, at Brevard County Government Center-North 518 South Palm Avenue, Brevard Room Titusville, Florida 32796 at 11:00 a.m., in accordance with Section 45.031, Florida Statutes. The Clerk of the Court shall not conduct said sale unless Plaintiff or Plaintiff's representative is present.

A pg. 23

DONE AND ORDERED in Chambers, at Brevard County, Florida, this 2_ [Hand Written]day of _Dec [Hand Written], 2009

s/ David Dugan [Signature Illegible]

CIRCUIT COURT JUDGE

Copies to:

Marlene L. Kirtland, Esq.
Becker & Poliakoff, P.A.
2500 Maitland Center Parkway, #209
Maitland, Florida 32751

Thomas Jewusiak
2835 Highway A1A North, Unit 901
Indialantic, FL 32903

IN THE DISTRICT COURT OF APPEAL OF THE STATE OF FLORIDA FIFTH DISTRICT
JANUARY TERM 2012
[Rubber Stamp] NOT FINAL UNTIL THE TIME EXPIRES TO FILE REHEARING MOTION, AND IF FILED, DISPOSED OF.

THOMAS JEWUSIAK,

Appellant,

v.   Case No. 5D10-98

SANDY KAYE CONDOMINIUM ASSOCIATION, INC.

Appellee.

_____/

Decision filed   January 31, 2012

Appeal from the Circuit Court
for Brevard County,
David Dugan, Judge.

Thomas Jewusiak, Indialantic, pro se.
Lilliana M. Farinas-Sabogal, of Becker & Poliakoff, P.A. Miami, for Appellee.

PER CURIAM
AFFIRMED

EVANDER, COHEN and JACOBUS, JJ, concur

IN THE DISTRICT COURT OF APPEAL OF THE
STATE OF FLORIDA FIFTH DISTRICT

THOMAS JEWUSIAK,
Appellant,

v.   CASE NO. 5D10-98

SANDY KAYE CONDOMINIUM
ASSOCIATION, INC,
Appellee.
_____/

DATE March 1, 2012

BY ORDER OF THE COURT:

ORDERED that Appellant's Motion Requesting that this Court Rehear and Reconsider its Decision and or Clarify its Decision and or Render an Opinion in this Matter, filed February 15, 2012, is denied.

I hereby certify that the foregoing is
(a true copy of) the original Court order.
[Seal]: DISTRICT COURT OF APPEAL STATE OF FLORIDA

s/ Pamela R. Masters

PAMELA R MASTERS, CLERK

cc Thomas Jewusiak

Supreme Court of Florida

TUESDAY, MAY 1, 2012

CASE NO.: SC12-692
Lower Tribunal No(s).: 5D10-98,

05-2006-CA-52659

THOMAS JEWUSIAK

vs. SANDY KAYE

A pg. 28

CONDOMINIUM ASSOCIATION, INC.

Petitioner(s)   Respondent(s)

    Having determined that this Court is without jurisdiction, this case is hereby dismissed. See Jackson v. State, 926 So. 2nd 1262 (Fla. 2006); Jenkins v. State, 385 So. 2d 1356 (Fla. 1980). No motion for rehearing will be entertained by this Court.
A True Copy
Test:

s/Thomas D. Hall__ [Seal] SUPREME COURT
Thomas D. Hall   OF THE STATE OF FLORIDA
Clerk, Supreme Court

kb
Served:
HON. PAMELA R. MASTERS, CLERK
THOMAS JEWUSIAK
LILLIANA M. FARINAS-SABOGAL
HON. MITCH NEEDELMAN, CLERK
HON. WILLIAM DAVID DUGAN, JUDGE

A pg. 29

No. 12-180

In the

Supreme Court of the United States

Thomas G. Jewusiak, *Petitioner*

v.

Sandy Kaye Condominium Association, Inc.,
Respondents

On Petition for Writ of Certiorari to the Florida Fifth
District Court of Appeal

PETITION FOR REHEARING

Thomas G. Jewusiak
P.O. Box 33794
Indialantic Florida 32903
321-292-2450
Jewusiak1@aol.com

November 22, 2012

Table of Contents

TABLE OF CONTENTS............................(i)-(iv)

TABLE OF AUTHORITIES........................ (v)-(vii)

THE CASE FOR REHEARING 1-14

1. The refusal of the Florida courts to obey the law, the procedures as laid down in the trilogy of federal cases, *Celotex*, *Matushita* and *Anderson*, is, in itself, a violation of due process.. 1

2. Rule 56 is grounded in the Constitution, as it must be; it is encoded in federal law and its violation is a U.S. Constitutional violation where matters of life, "liberty" or "property" are concerned.. 1

3. To the extent it mirrors rule 56, Florida's own rule 1.510 encodes in Florida law the protections of the United States Constitution.............................1

4. In the case at issue the Florida courts have not committed a simple error in interpreting its own rules, rather it has violated its rules; broken its own law.. 2

(ii)

5. The fact that Florida promulgated rules and procedures and then ignored those same rules and procedures is itself a violation of due process where life, "liberty" or "property" is concerned.. 2

6. Due process means the rule of law, the law of the land... 3

7. "Fairness of procedure is 'due process in the primary sense.'".. 6

8. It is by means of examining the due process protections afforded those subject to non-judicial administrative hearings, which involve the deprivation of fundamental rights, that we can better understand the due process rights within a judicial setting 7

9. The extent to which procedural due process must be afforded is influenced by the extent to which the recipient may be 'condemned to suffer grievous loss'... 8

10. Due process depends upon whether the recipient's interest in avoiding the loss outweighs the governmental interest in summary adjudication... 8

11. In almost every setting where important decisions turn on questions of fact, due process

requires an opportunity to confront and cross-examine adverse witnesses............................. 9

12. There was no competent evidence submitted by Sandy Kaye so the judge heard and accepted the hearsay "testimony" of Sandy Kaye's counsel without allowing cross-examination 10

13. The judge, though not permitted under the rules of summary judgment to take testimony, did so, and proclaimed his findings of fact in his summary judgment order.. 10

14. In administrative hearings it is imperative that the agency not only follow its own rules but it must demonstrate how it reaches its conclusions and on what basis in its own rules
.... 11

15. Thomas Jewusiak invoked the United States constitutional claim when he demanded a trial by Jury which was denied without legal rationale or citation of law... 13

16. Although it is accepted that the Seventh Amendment to the Bill of Right has not been extended to the states in civil trials it is also accepted that when a state takes on that right in its own constitution it is not permitted to

deny that right without violating the U.S. Constitution..13

17. This Supreme Court may choose to intervene if a lower court "has so far departed from the accepted and usual course of judicial proceedings or sanctioned such departure of a lower court, as to call for an exercise of this Court's supervisory power." The Brevard Florida Court is an outlaw court that has violated its own laws and procedures 14

CONCLUSION..14

TABLE OF AUTHORITIES

BOARD OF GOVERNORS OF UNIVERSITY OF NC, 704 F. 2d 713 (4th Cir. 1983)........................ 2

Brinkerhoff-Faris Co. v. Hill, 281 U. S. 673, 681 S.Ct. 7

Broward County v La Rosa, 484 So.2d 1374 (Fla. 4th DCA 1986) 14

Cafeteria & Restaurant Workers Union v. McElroy, 367 U. S. 886, 895 S.Ct.(1961) 9

Chapman v. California, 386 US 18 S.Ct. (1967)..... 3

E. g., ICC v. Louisville & N. R. Co., 227 U. S. 88, 93-94 S.Ct.(1913).. 9

Goldberg v. Kelly, 397 US 254 S.Ct. (1970) ... 8, 9, 12

Greene v. McElroy, 360 U.S. 474, 496-497 S.Ct.(1959) 9,10

Hannah v. Larche, 363 U. S. 420, 440, 442 S.Ct.(1960) 9

Joint Anti-Fascist Refugee Comm. v. McGrath, 341 US 123 S.Ct. (1951) 7, 6

Leslie v. Attorney General of US, 611 F. 3d 171 3rd Cir. (2010) 12

Murray's Lessee v. Hoboken Land & Improv. Co., 18 How. 272, 276 (1856).. 6

Ohio Bell Tel. Co. v. PUC, 301 U. S. 292 S.Ct.(1937) 12

Olmstead v. United States, 277 US 438 S.Ct.(1928) 13

Pryse Monument Co. v. District Court, Etc., Okl., 595 P.2d 435, 438 (1979) 7

The Printing House, Inc. v. State Dept. of Revenue, 614 So. 2d 1119, 1123 (Fla.1stDCA 1992).............. 14

United States v. Abilene & S. R. Co., 265 U. S. 274, 288-289 S.Ct.(1924).. 12

United States v. Caceres, 440 U.S. 741, 752-53 & n. 15, 99 S.Ct. 1465, 1472 & n. 15, 59 L.Ed.2d 733 (1979) 3

Wichita R. & Light Co. v. PUC, 260 U. S. 48, 57-59 S.Ct.(1922) 12

Willner v. Committee on Character & Fitness, 373 U. S. 96, 103-104 S.Ct.(1963)................................... 9

1 Annals of Cong. 439 (1789)............................... 4

Coke's Institutes, Second Part, 50 (1st ed. 1642) 5

Magna Carta signed by King John (1215) 5

Statutory rendition of the *Magna Carta* A.D. 1354 during the reign of Edward III 5

FED. R.CIV. P. 56.................................. 1, 2, 8, 11

Fla. R. Civ. P. 1.510..................................... 1, 11

Fifth and Fourteenth Amendments to the Constitution of the United States...1, 2, 3, 4, 5, 6, 7, 8, 9, 12, 14

Seventh Amendment to the Constitution of the United States.. 13

Florida Constitution, Article 1, Section 22 13

This Petition for Rehearing shall incorporate within it, by reference, Thomas Jewusiak's Petition For Writ Of Certiorari.

The questions presented in that Petition, numbered one and two, are repetitive. As is made clear within the questions, **1. the refusal of the Florida courts to obey the law, the procedures as laid down in the trilogy of federal cases, *Celotex*, *Matushita* and *Anderson*, is, in itself, a violation of due process.** Asking whether a citizen can have his home seized without due process is equivalent to asking whether the Florida Courts can refuse to obey the rules of summary judgment as interpreted by *Celotex*, *Matushita* and *Anderson* and thereby violate due process.

The trilogy is the Court's attempt to preserve due process while "streamlining" court procedure by means of summary judgment. **2. Rule 56 is grounded in the Constitution, as it must be; it is encoded in federal law and its violation is a U.S. Constitutional violation where matters of life, "liberty" or "property" are concerned.**

3. To the extent it mirrors rule 56, Florida's own rule 1.510 encodes in Florida law the protections of the United States Constitution, as many a Florida judge reminds us. That Florida's rule 1.510 affords greater protection, (as interpreted by the Florida courts), than federal rule 56, is noteworthy, remaining cognizant of the fact that if the Florida courts fall below the standards of Rule 56, as interpreted by the federal courts, they are in violation of the of the United States Constitution.

4. In the case at issue the Florida courts have not committed a simple error in interpreting its own rules, rather it has violated its rules, broken its own law, with an abandon that takes the breath away.

Even if they were not grounded in the United States Constitution, as they most certainly are, (in so far as they mirror Rule 56 **5. the fact that Florida promulgated rules and procedures and then with an unbounded arrogance ignored those same rules and procedures is itself a violation of due process**. Again, we are not talking about mere error or a subtle misinterpretation; we have in the case at issue a, wholesale, disregard of law, law that is well established; of a lower tribunal that has taken upon itself the power to become a law unto itself, of a court that has no fear of being overruled or superintended by any other authority.

The responsibility of a state court to follow its own law and procedures when they embody U. S. Constitutional principles is clear in *Jones v. BOARD OF GOVERNORS OF UNIVERSITY OF NC, 704 F. 2d 713 (4th Cir 1983)*:

> "...[T]o the extent a state's procedures directly embody fundamental guarantees grounded in the due process clause, a significant departure from those procedures would as well violate

> the underlying constitutionally based guarantees. Furthermore, there persists in controlling decisions of the Supreme Court recognition that significant departures from stated procedures of government ... if sufficiently unfair and prejudicial, constitute procedural due process violations, see *United States v. Caceres*, 440 U.S. 741, 752-53 & n. 15, 99 S.Ct. 1465, 1472 & n. 15, 59 L.Ed.2d 733 (1979)."

Chapman v. California, 386 US 18 S.Ct.(1967):

> [R]ights guaranteed against invasion by the Fifth and Fourteenth Amendments, [are] rights rooted in the Bill of Rights, offered and championed in the Congress by James Madison, who told the Congress that the "independent" federal courts would be the "guardians of those rights." ... With faithfulness to the constitutional union of the States, we cannot leave to the States the formulation of the authoritative laws, rules, and remedies designed to protect people from infractions by the States of federally guaranteed rights."

Further quoting Madison:

> "If they [the first ten amendments] are incorporated into the Constitution, independent tribunals of justice will consider themselves in a peculiar manner the

guardians of those rights; they will be an impenetrable bulwark against every assumption of power in the Legislative or Executive; they will be naturally led to resist every encroachment upon rights expressly stipulated for in the Constitution by the declaration of rights." *1 Annals of Cong.* 439 (1789).

It is a national tragedy that Madison's promise of a court of final appeal, an impenetrable bulwark, a Supreme Court, has been abandoned in the name of judicial economy; that the Court we have hears cases only at their secret discretion; that the overwhelming majority of cases never making it past the desk of an overworked clerk.

6. Due process means the rule of law, the law of the land. Clause 39 of Magna Carta:

> "No free man shall be seized or imprisoned, or stripped of his rights or possessions, or outlawed or exiled, or deprived of his standing in any other way, nor will we proceed with force against him, or send others to do so, except by the lawful judgment of his equals or by the law of the land." The text of Magna Carta signed by King John (1215)

The phrase due process of law appeared in a statutory rendition of the Magna Carta in A.D. 1354 during the reign of Edward III:

> "No man of what state or condition he be, shall be put out of his lands or tenements nor taken, nor disinherited, nor put to death, without he be brought to answer by due process of law."

Lord Coke, in 1642, concluded "due process of law" meant "by law of the land." *Coke's Institutes, Second Part*, 50 (1st ed. 1642).

An early Supreme Court interpreting the Due Process Clause declared " '[t]he words, "due process of law", were undoubtedly intended to convey the same meaning as the words "by the law of the land' " in Magna Charta." *Murray's Lessee v. Hoboken Land & Improv. Co.*, 18 How. 272, 276 (1856).

We have progressed little in 750 years. We are plagued, not by kings, but by tyrannical courts; we are arbitrarily and violently dispossessed, not by the king's armed, mounted men, wielding truncheons, but by a Brevard county sheriff fingering his Glock.

(I use the term "we" advisedly. If one person can have his property forcibly seized by the state without due process then no person's property is safe from arbitrary taking.)

Justice William Douglas rose to eloquence:

> "Due process is perhaps the most majestic concept in our whole constitutional system. While it contains the garnered wisdom of the past in assuring fundamental justice, it is also

a living principle not confined to past instances." *Joint Anti-Fascist Refugee Comm. v. McGrath* 341 US 123 S.Ct. (1951)

Repeatedly when speaking of due process we hear the phrases fundamental justice, fairness of procedure. One cannot formulate rules of procedure only to have them ignored at a judge's whim.

> 7. **"Fairness of procedure is 'due process in the primary sense.'"** *Brinkerhoff-Faris Co. v. Hill*, 281 U. S. 673, 681.

Due process cannot be achieved without adherence to established law and procedure. The Oklahoma Supreme citing the United States Supreme Court framed it succinctly:

> "Fundamental fairness in litigation process cannot be afforded except within a framework of orderly procedure. No area of the law may lay claim to exemption from the range of its basic strictures ... Chaos, caprice and ad hoc pronouncements would inevitably follow from any departure." *Pryse Monument Co. v. District Court, Etc., Okl.,* 595 P.2d 435, 438 (1979) which quotes:

> " ... It is procedure that spells much of the difference between rule by law and rule by whim or caprice. Steadfast adherence to strict procedural safeguards is our main assurance that there will be equal justice under law. .."

Joint Anti-Fascist Refugee Committee v. McGrath, 341 U.S. 123, 179, 71 S.Ct. 624, 652, 95 L.Ed. 817 (1951) (Douglas, J., concurring)"

They left out one of Douglas's most important points: "It is not without significance that most of the provisions of the Bill of Rights are procedural."

It is instructive to approach the issue of the denial of due process as if the protections of Rule 56 and the case law interpreting it did not exist; as if Rule 56 did not enshrine fundamental, due process rights; as if it were not fundamentally a rule protecting the Constitution.

8. It is by means of examining the extraordinary due process protections afforded those subject to non-judicial administrative hearings, which involve the deprivation of fundamental rights, that we can better understand the due process rights within a judicial setting, when the seizure of a person's home is involved.

It is in a case involving the termination of welfare benefits in *Goldberg v. Kelly*, 397 US 254 S.Ct.(1970):

> 9. "**The extent to which procedural due process must be afforded the recipient is influenced by the extent to which he may be 'condemned to suffer grievous loss,'** " quoting from *Joint Anti-Fascist Refugee Committee v. McGrath*, 341

U. S. 123, 168 (1951) (Frankfurter, J., concurring),

What more "grievous loss" may a person suffer that the loss of his home and all his assets, except, perhaps, for the loss of his life.

The Supreme Court further stated in *Goldberg v. Kelly:* 10. **Due process**

> "....**depends upon whether the recipient's interest in avoiding that loss outweighs the governmental interest in summary adjudication.** Accordingly, as we said in *Cafeteria & Restaurant Workers Union v. McElroy*, 367 U. S. 886, 895 S.Ct.(1961), 'consideration of what procedures due process may require under any given set of circumstances must begin with a determination of the precise nature of the government function involved as well as of the private interest that has been affected by governmental action.'" See also *Hannah v. Larche*, 363 U. S. 420, 440, 442 S.Ct.(1960)

What did the state have to gain in depriving Thomas Jewusiak of his only home and all his assets? Why did the lower tribunal become the obedient servant of Sandy Kaye if it had no financial stake in the forcible taking of these assets?

As stated further in *Goldberg v. Kelly*, 397 US 254 S.Ct.(1970):

11. "In almost every setting where important decisions turn on questions of fact, due process requires an opportunity to confront and cross-examine adverse witnesses. *E. g., ICC v. Louisville & N. R. Co.*, 227 U. S. 88, 93-94 S.Ct.(1913); *Willner v. Committee on Character & Fitness*, 373 U. S. 96, 103-104 S.Ct.(1963). What we said in *Greene v. McElroy*, 360 U. S. 474, 496-497 S.Ct.(1959), is particularly pertinent here:

> 'Certain principles have remained relatively immutable in our jurisprudence. One of these is that where governmental action seriously injures an individual, and the reasonableness of the action depends on fact findings, the evidence used to prove the Government's case must be disclosed to the individual so that he has an opportunity to show that it is untrue. While this is important in the case of documentary evidence, it is even more important where the evidence consists of the testimony of individuals whose memory might be faulty or who, in fact, might be perjurers or persons motivated by malice, vindictiveness, intolerance, prejudice, or jealousy. We have formalized these protections in the requirements of confrontation and

cross-examination. They have ancient roots. They find expression in the Sixth Amendment . . . . This Court has been zealous to protect these rights from erosion. It has spoken out not only in criminal cases, . . . but also in all types of cases where administrative. . . actions were under scrutiny.' "

That the lower tribunal judge in the case at issue was not permitted under rule 1.510 to take testimony and conduct a trial of the facts did not prevent him from doing just that. 12. **There was no competent evidence submitted by Sandy Kaye so the judge heard and accepted the hearsay "testimony" of Sandy Kaye's counsel.** Needless to say, Thomas Jewusiak was not allowed to cross-examine this hearsay witness at "trial". 13. **The fact that the judge was not permitted under the rules of summary judgment to make determinations of fact did not prevent the lower tribunal judge from doing exactly that. In fact, quite astoundingly, he issued his, so-called, findings of fact in his summary judgment order.** This was a judge that had absolutely no fear of appellate review and rightfully so, because there was no possibility of real review.

It is made clear in rule 56 and Florida's rule 1.510 that a judge in rendering his summary judgment decision must address each affirmative defense raised in opposition to summary judgment and state his reasons for reaching his judgment. **In the case at** issue no Florida court has ever given any legal rationale or basis for the conclusions it has reached. It is as if the rules of summary judgment did not exist. The Fifth District issued no opinion thereby making it bullet proof, unappealable to the Florida Supreme Court. The fact that there is no right to appeal to the United States Supreme Court is self-evident by the very necessity of this document.

14. **In administrative hearings it is imperative that the agency not only follow its own rules but it must demonstrate how it reaches its conclusions and on what basis in its own rules.**

It is once again in *Goldberg v Kelly*:

> "Finally, the decision maker's conclusion as to a recipient's eligibility must rest solely on the legal rules and evidence adduced at the hearing. *Ohio Bell Tel. Co. v. PUC*, 301 U. S. 292 S.Ct.(1937); *United States v. Abilene & S. R. Co.*, 265 U. S. 274, 288-289 S.Ct.(1924). To demonstrate compliance with this elementary requirement, **the decision maker should state the reasons for his determination and indicate the evidence he relied on.**' cf. *Wichita R. & Light Co. v. PUC,* 260 U. S. 48, 57-59 S.Ct.(1922)"

Leslie v. Attorney General of US, 611 F. 3d 171 3rd Cir.(2010):

> " '[t]he notion of fair play animating [the Fifth Amendment [and the Fourteenth]] precludes an agency from promulgating a regulation affecting individual liberty or interest, which the rule-maker may then with impunity ignore or disregard as it sees fit' *Montilla*, 926 F.2d at 164. We believe that a rule distinguishing regulatory rights that are statutorily or constitutionally grounded from those that are born purely of regulations comports with these precepts."

I would argue that where an agency or court disregards or ignores its own laws and procedures and thus becomes an "outlaw" court or agency, that fact, in itself, raises it to constitutional due process issue in cases where life, liberty or property hang in the balance.

Olmstead v. United States, 277 US 438 S.Ct.(1928):

> "In a government of laws, existence of the government will be imperiled if it fails to observe the law scrupulously…. Crime is contagious. If the Government becomes a lawbreaker, it breeds contempt for law; it invites every man to become a law unto himself."

15. Thomas Jewusiak invoked the United States constitutional claim when he demanded a trial by Jury which was denied without legal rationale or citation of law (See A pg.1 in "Petition"). **16.**

Although it is accepted that the Seventh Amendment to the Bill of Right has not been extended to the states in civil trials it is also accepted that when a state takes on that right in its own constitution it is not permitted to deny that right without violating the U.S. Constitution.

The first article of Florida's Constitution contains the state's bill of rights which reflects the United States Bill of Rights, elaborated to further reflect the judgments of the United States Supreme Court. It states that all rights granted must be consistent with U.S. Supreme Court's interpretation of those rights in the federal constitution.

The *Florida Constitution*, Article 1, Section 22: "The right of trial by jury shall be secure to all and remain inviolate." The right exists for those issues that were triable before a jury at common law at the time of the adoption of Florida's first constitution. *Broward County v La Rosa*, 484 So.2d 1374 (Fla. 4th DCA 1986) It is also extended to "proceedings of like nature" as those under the rules of common law. *The Printing House, Inc. v. State Dept. of Revenue,* 614 So. 2d 1119, 1123 (Fla.1st DCA 1992).

As argued herein, within the framework of due process, it applies equally here; Florida cannot promulgate rules and laws rooted in the United States Constitution and break those laws at will; it cannot guarantee the right to trial by jury in civil cases and then violate that guarantee with impunity.

CONCLUSION

I ask that this Court fulfill its title and rise to the occasion, uphold the dream of James Madison, that it be, a guardian, an impenetrable bulwark in defense of the Constitution, a true appeals court, a Supreme Court.

We hear dying echoes of Madison in this Court's Rule 10 which "although neither controlling nor fully measuring the Court's discretion, indicate the character of the reasons the Court considers."

17. This Court may choose to intervene if a lower court "has so far departed from the accepted and usual course of judicial proceedings or sanctioned such departure of a lower court, as to call for an exercise of this Court's supervisory power."

The Brevard Florida Court is an outlaw court that has violated its own laws and procedures. It is not only Thomas Jewusiak who has had his home taken in violation of the Constitution but others who have had their lives ruined and their cases buried by essentially unappealable orders issued without legal rationale or foundation.

One family may have absolutely no importance to this Court; but this Court must serve notice so that countless others will be spared destruction from the outlaw courts of this land.

I appeal to a vision possessed by James Madison and the founders of this country; that their dream not be allowed to die.

CERTIFICATE OF GOOD FAITH

No.12-180

Thomas G. Jewusiak,

                              Petitioner

v.

Sandy Kaye Condominium Association,

                              Respondents

As required by Supreme Court Rule 44.2, I certify that the The Petition For Rehearing the Petition For Writ Of Certiorari is restricted to the grounds specified in Rule 44.2 which in plain language specifies "or other substantial grounds not previously presented". This Petition is presented in good faith and not for delay.

I declare under penalty of perjury that the foregoing is true and correct.

Executed on November 22, 2012

Thomas G. Jewusiak, pro se

P. O. Box 33794

Indialantic, Florida 32903

321-292-2450 jewusiak1@aol.com

www.ingramcontent.com/pod-product-compliance
Lightning Source LLC
LaVergne TN
LVHW050630090426
835512LV00007B/770